To, Sharon
Thank

CW00408281

+

Solace
For
Salem

Enjoy!

Tiegan Marie

Tiegan Marie

DEDICATION

For my parents, my grandparents, and for my partner, and friends. Thank you for always supporting me, thank you for everything.

CONTENTS

Introduction   i

Welcome to Salem   1

Bridget Bishop: The First Witch   3

The Gown and the Gallows   4

Sarah and Dorothy Good: Is there any Good in Salem?   5

The Devil and Her Daughters   6

Elizabeth Howe: Howe You Accuse Us   7

Susannah Martin: Salisbury to Salem   8

Rebecca Nurse: Rumours   9

Sarah Wildes: The Wilde Accusation   10

George Burroughs: Subservient   11

Martha Carrier: Falsehood so Filthy   12

John Willard: Moralities   13

George Jacobs Sr: The Colour Red   14

John Proctor: Maroon   15

Alice Parker: The Inevitable   16

Mary Parker: Dreaming   17

Wilmot Redd: Fairy-tale Town   19

Margaret Scott: Missing   20

Samuel Wardwell: The Red String   21

Martha Corey: Until Death   22

Mary Easty: Helix   23

Ann Pudeator: Futility   24

Giles Corey: Tranquility   25

Present Day: The Weeping Wiccan Writes   26

The Modern Murderers   28

About the Author   29

INTRODUCTION

The following collection aims to honour the lives of individuals who have unjustly and tragically lost their lives, whether it be through the Salem witch trials or through other unfortunate circumstances. May they all find eternal happiness and peace.

WELCOME TO SALEM

The crows bicker and whine
Watching our empty graves stand tall
Sprouting into history books
Of works of fables and fiction
Polished and pristine
Our administered legacy.

Tourists flood the sacred grounds
Desperate to see the etched engravings
To gawk at hollow marble slabs
Ignorant to the ache behind them
To the anguish they represent
Their footsteps stain the soil
Yet, no bodies lie underneath.

A modern world where victims lie
Where liberation is a capital crime
Millions upon millions die
Barely seen on fleeting feeds
A scroll, a like, a dry cold eye
A modern world where people die.

Another unmarked plot of land
Another soul designed to suffer
Another shallow marble tab
To mark the tourist's sunken soil.

When the church bell tolls in Salem
Our remains shiver and shudder
You thank God for the death of prejudice
When really
That bell just marks another.

BRIDGET BISHOP:

THE FIRST WITCH

I wore sunflowers to match the sunset
But you saw serpent eyes
I wore thistles to match my garden
Yet you saw poisonous lies
I wore baneberries to match the roses
You saw the Devil in my hem.

The lakes that fill in Salem
Well, they used to sparkle blue
Now they shine with crimson
My gown drips with it too.

My name was Bridget Bishop
The first witch of my kind
But not one you'd read in fairy tales
One by powerful men, defined
They hung me from a tree that day
And from the oak, I swung
June 10th, 1692
An innocent woman hung.

THE GOWN AND THE GALLOWS

The blue bead lilies at my waist
Turning my dress to sunset shades
I found my nurture within nature
My pigment in its plants
The herbs became a home
A speck of colour in my sepia town
From a hue to a heartless end.

My once-blue dress just sits there
Stained with the Liverleaf I found
The Sunrise shades, not dyed, just drip
The crimson against their rope.

The flowers in my pot still sit there
As the black metal tin just swings
Along with my lifeless body
As the crowd at the gallows sings.

SARAH AND DOROTHY GOOD:

IS THERE ANY GOOD IN SALEM?

When your child begins to bite
Be careful whom you tell
Lock your doors up tight
Or you'll feel the wrath of Hell.

Your child begins to cry and revel
And you know you can't save her
You may think these men the devil
But they're all labelled Salem's saviours.

In her eyes a speck of crimson
The Devils' shade of red
Their sickness blamed on women
Their morality misled.

To prosecute Sarah Good
They took her infant's tale
Her poverty misunderstood
Her new-born dead in jail.

THE DEVIL AND HER DAUGHTERS

To what would've been my Mercy
If only some were shown
I hope like Bridget's flowers
In the gates of heaven you've grown.

To Dorothy my descendant
At the gates of heaven I wait
holding my arms out wide for you
My forgiveness I hope you take
It is the prejudice of Salem
That my heart will forever hate.

ELIZABETH HOWE:

HOWE YOU ACCUSE US

Would an omniscient God not know her place?
Would the thunder you see in her eyes not require a
storm?
I hath proclaimed my innocence and walked up to
prove it so
My gaze bewitched the accuser
You ask me, yet I do not know.

Would the powerful witch before you
Not execute some control?
Would the Bishop you seek to guide you
Not have read scriptures of me before?

Yet the power you fear doth scare you
And the sicknesses you can't explain
So, you stand in front of the Jury
Elizabeth Howe, you blame.

SUSANNAH MARTIN:

SALISBURY TO SALEM

I saw my life as a clock
One that would constantly tick
The man-made hands stretched out to mine
My heart pumped blood at their will
In 1692 they came for me
After my dear George had died
He who had once stopped their persecution
Was no longer by my side
The clock struck twelve when they buried him
The village all gathered to cry
Yet as my body hung from the gallows
Not one tear shed from their eyes
And the grave next to George they'd promised me
Was just another lie.

REBECCA NURSE:

RUMOURS

I was once deemed a remarkable citizen
Held in such prestige,
Lived in a place where I was adored,
Until the rumours spread
Some accused the Putnam family
But alas the final verdict was read
I left behind eight children
When they hung me at Proctor's Ledge
A once valued member of society
Discarded, left for dead.

SARAH WILDES:

THE WILDE ACCUSATION

Red scarf hung round my neck
Temptation for my arrest
The colour of love turned violent
My marriage was the start of death
I clung to the red scarves fibres
And imagined what I could
That my husband John was holding me
That Salem understood.

When my time had all descended
And the hourglass tipped out
They took my red scarf from me
From the jail cell I did shout.

I kissed my John goodbye that day
But yet, I knew our love would live
"An angel sent too soon" God said
As the noose caressed my neck
My red scarf finally came to me
But fabric it was not
For when my blood pooled under my skin
My new red scarf would rot.

GEORGE BURROUGHS:

SUBSERVIENT

"Tell me what to do?"
I asked unto the Lord
I leant my ear to his spirit
For his gold flecked scriptures to croon
Like a shepherd to the night star
To lend me his good tongue, I begged
For his omniscience to save the day
For him to slow the sun
Stop time where it stood
And I would be his Shepherd
But my prayer was misunderstood
No crook caressed my arms, no shear to reap the wool
My role was not to serve
But to keep their stomachs full.

MARTHA CARRIER:

FALSEHOOD SO FILTHY

Smallpox got my family
Salem took the rest
The little life left around me
Captured after my arrest
I fought to prove my innocence
But the "Victims" did persist
My own Son turned against me
My only crime was to exist.

JOHN WILLARD:

MORALITIES

Say my name before death calls me
Remember who knocked at his door
For it was not I who wished for his visit
I realised the wrongs of those shallow graves
Protesting, I gave up my work
No blood be on my hands
In death, I cleaned them
Better to die a witch than to kill for dubious virtue.

Watch the crows of Salem gather
If the birds still be well
Or have you condemned them to the same fate
Do their feathers rest in hell?
Will my tombstone bring a crowd?
Or will the bleak mass gather elsewhere
To watch another be killed.

They may not visit my grave
But soon they too will be condemned to the ground
Willard be the name they cry
As the flames of hell doth burn
Alongside the ash of righteousness
Their afterlife, a spilled urn.

GEORGE JACOBS SR:

THE COLOUR RED

Red I saw when angry
Red, my knuckles bruised
Red was the morning fit of rage I felt
Against the evening twilight plum.

Red I saw with love
When my daughter bore a child
Red was when my heart did glow
Like the winter dusk born stars.

But alas no Red Devil at my death
Their lies were never true
For what I saw on Proctor's Ledge
When I drew my final breath
As the golden sun shone down on me
George Jacobs Sr laid to rest
Draped in peaceful summer blue.

JOHN PROCTOR:

MAROON

A hill dripping red
Against the midnight canvas hue
A place where the blood moon would always rise
Where empty plots of soil waited to be filled.

On tabs of stone, they carved our names
Acid running through rotting veins
Their words like poison
Contaminating remains
"Ann Putnam, who hurt you?"
I hear the court cry
"Goodman Proctor and his wife too",
Our lives ruined with a lie.

A defeated expedition to heal one's home
In equity I lost the war
For when I tried to save them all
My body was dragged away
Taking the same scarlet trail
That the other 'witches' laid.

ALICE PARKER:

THE INEVITABLE

"Not I!" said Alice, but she already knew
Evidence was futile and the verdict was due
"Vile and venom" their tongues did spit
Eyes burned into backs
Another conflict.

A burning sensation warmed their bones
Their bruised limbs berating
Burning down homes
Beckoning for the rise of a regime
An idea no longer confined to our dreams.

In the air we remained as a spectre to see
Gawk at your Justice as you spill your bile
For thee, the treatment will be no less than hostile
Greeted by your demons with a devilish smile
In death we will meet again.

Bitter, burnt, black but brief
None of Salem will understand our grief
In this Blood-thirsty barren
Our vengeance reigns on
As we mourn for eternity
A life incomplete.

MARY PARKER:

DREAMING

No ocean stood near me, but I imagined the waves
The way the gentle blue would caress the sand
How each pebble would skip so perfectly along the
shore
The crashing of waves would fill my ears
Ignorant to the bitter breeze that Salem had borne
Reality was gone.

The name they called me is not mine
Yet it is my hands that seem to be bound
As I look over the ledge for someone else's crime
My thoughts drift to the marina's sounds.

I imagined what it would be like to feel the sand against
my feet
To feel the sharpened pebbles poke my skin
The cuts creating a scarlet trail as I approached the
waves
Eventually soothed by the sea's salt ridden marine
What I would give to absorb the beauty of nature
Like a cut to the sea.

But soon, my daydream would end
All eight of us would approach the stand
Silence.
The echo of the waves would leave me
The bitter breeze would take flight
Our cart would soon be free
Its wheels would carry me to my eternal slumber
With hope of an everlasting dream.

The cliff edge would turn to Proctor's
The shoreline fantasy would fade
The sand would turn back to soil
My deathbed would be made
And the seashell necklace laid upon my collar
Would become nothing but a callous cut of rope.

WILMOT REDD:

FAIRY-TALE TOWN

A bloody cleaver in a baby's cot
A cart that wouldn't pull
These rumours piled against me
To fill an executioner's debt
Appeasing prosecutors meant to protect
A benevolent village they sought
Where the trees were fruitless but full
Where the vines were beige
And hung like snakes
Dangling the innocence caught
The trees with a crimson hue
The tainted stream that grew thicker
A place where water barely resided
Where "witches" blood dyed their bricks
Where executioners were liberators
Living was a luxury
A failed wish.

MARGARET SCOTT:

MISSING

They could never find any documents
No warrant for my arrest
Just scattered scarlet leading up to the ledge
Only a memorial with an etched name
My poverty was my crime
My dependence, a mark of death
A witch is what they called me
"A witch?" is what I asked
Surely if I had magic
I'd have escaped this dratted past.

In my dreams I ran away from here
No court case would greet me
But instead, a summer night
Washing myself with nature
Disregarding a futile plight
No executioners would dare cross me
No rope would touch my skin
My wish to be away from the gallows
My wish to wash away their sin.

SAMUEL WARDWELL:

THE RED STRING

They said I was one with the Devil
So, in desperation, to find him I tried
If their words spoke of my misdeeds
Maybe he could help
The book of his great horns
His fire-marked skin
The brush of an infant's cry that caressed his brow
Each feature wound with misery
The feeling of death as companion and foe.

They said that God rejected me
That witchcraft soaked my blood
That through the cloths of time
An entity would meet me
Alas, I remained alone.

Rejected from the Gods above
Thunder spitting down
Locked out from hell's fiery gates
Turned away from the angels
A life cut short
By morality's blade
"Seat me next to the one whom loves me"
But no such seat ever came
I made a home in purgatory
A home I eagerly wait to leave.

MARTHA COREY:

UNTIL DEATH

If my frozen flesh in winter was given just a peek
To witness the hatching dismal stems
Pining for their petals over a frost-bitten leaf
A reminder of what once was
Shall the stem give up too?
Or long for their return?
Reminiscing on the memory of colour
Of the shades lost to the summer breeze.

My own husband turned against me
Inviting Death to our door
Our halted seed lost to sleet
My winter stem
His bitter breeze
In vows he surely lied
The one meant to protect me
Now the reason that I died.

MARY EASTY:

HELIX

My DNA is what killed me
The puritan mould did crack
My double helix
A twisted strand
The molecule that formed a life
The very structure that bore me
Tore my life apart
By the Jury of Salem's verdict
I was vermin from the start.

ANN PUDEATOR:

FUTILITY

The frosted tips
The winter rain
The sweat that gathered on my brow
The way each loss stained the fibres
The way the rope would never not swing
Fresh to an execution's bout.

The morning summer dew
The break of dawn against the eve of dusk
Confined by a barricaded view
Ah, what it was like to be human
Simplicities of what I once knew.

A water droplet replaced by mist
A witches pow'r that didn't exist
We sat
We reminisced.

Lock ourselves inside we did
Away from the natural earth
Only fear caressed our cheeks that day
No summer breeze or frozen lakes
Just prejudice by a dying fire,
As the eight Firebrands did sway.

GILES COREY:

TRANQUILITY

Try me as they might
Their rocks, their boulders on my back
Each ounce crushes a bone
I was too late to save my Martha
Too late to save a broken home
So, if this is how God chooses to punish me
Remember the injustice of how I died
To go from slayer to slain
To die from excruciating pain
From one man to another:
You'll die just the same.

PRESENT DAY:

THE WEEPING WICCAN WRITES

I'm just a girl from modern England
A witch who wants to know
I wasn't born in Salem
Yet their tales struck me so.

I come from a line of Wiccans
We embrace the label "Witch"
We find our passion in our plants
We hold our herbs close to our heart.

Yes, the North may still seem lifeless
My dress may look quite glum
But if the blue bead lilies called to me
I know I won't be hung.

The breast that Dorothy fed from
Had cursed her from the start
The greatest misdeed that Sarah made
Was the miracle of birth.

My mother bore me to witchcraft
Her love was not unknown
And unlike the tale of the Goods'
Witchcraft became my home.

I think what really scares me
Is that these young women were killed
Killed in case their bloodline
Produced someone like me.

THE MODERN MURDERERS

It's the 21st Century now
Your devil horns turned to halos
As Wiccan Witches rise
Your death is seen as a tragedy
Your prosecutors despised.

Your bodies were never found, my dears
And I can't promise that we tried
But your story will be remembered
It's scattered here amongst these lines.

And this is for the younger ones
Who may not know your tale
The ones who think that executions
Are something you pass or fail
Look further than the test, my child
And search far and wide
Because I think you'll be surprised to find
That even modern people die.

ABOUT THE AUTHOR

Tiegan Marie is a contemporary author from the North of England, reading and writing Gothic, witchcraft, and fantasy literature in a tea-infused state.

On the rare occasions that she isn't sipping on a cup of tea, you can find her painting, writing, or daydreaming about her next adventure.

Solace for Salem is Tiegan's first book.

You can find Tiegan on Instagram and Twitter: @teapots_n_tales